GOLDEN HOMEMAKERS

Extensions and improvements

Marshall Cavendish London & New York

Introduction

Who can forecast with precision when he buys his home, what his circumstances will be five, ten, fifteen years later? Ideally, a house should be adaptable to changing family circumstances: additions to the family, perhaps; or a grandparent who moves in; a higher income that permits expansion of the house to cater for more ambitious entertaining, or the addition of a sun lounge, a study, a workroom, a rumpus room, a suite for teenagers.

This Golden Homemaker volume shows and explains 25 new house extensions and improvements and how each has been brought about. It incorporates hundreds of ideas that you can adapt to your own needs and wishes to 'add on' rather than move house. And the technical aspects of house extension are covered in the glossary at the back of the book.

Upwards and outwards!

Contents

25 New House Extensions and Improvements was prepared for Marshall Cavendish Limited by Gudenian, Rockail & Mayer Limited

© Marshall Cavendish Limited, 1972, 1976

Published by Marshall Cavendish Publications Limited, 58 Old Compton Street, London W1V 5PA

ISBN 0 85685 179 5

Printed in Great Britain Petty and Sons Limited, Leeds.

Key to plans: dining room, DR; dressing room, D; kitchen, K; living room, L; bedroom, BR; hall, H; work room, WR; hobby room, HR; lounge, LG; studio, S; bathroom, B; ground floor, GF; first floor FF; child's room, CR; store, ST; master bedroom, MBR; playroom, PR; basement, BM; toilet, T; garage, G; entrance, E; music room, MR; sliding glass doors, SGD.
Metric note: 6ft = 1.83m

EXTENSIONS
The First Principles

1 Any extension to a house that involves major constructional work is liable to be expensive. Before embarking on ambitious building plans such as the addition of a wing alongside or of a new storey upwards, make certain that these are viable for you from a financial point of view. Will you get your money back if, at a later date, you sell the house? In all probability, yes — and more than your money back. But might it make better financial sense to sell your present home and buy or build one to meet your expanding requirements?

2 Investigate the pros and cons of all systems and types of extension before reaching a decision. If you need more living space, it may be feasible and relatively uncostly to extend into the attic or cellar, assuming your house has one or the other. If you do want to build on, consider the possibilities of a prefabricated unit, which is usually cheaper to add than an architect-designed custom-built extension.

3 In the case of any major constructional project, call on the expertise of the professionals — unless you are confident of your own technical and practical skills. You may decide to employ a building firm to do the job without benefit of independent professional advice. If so, procure itemized estimates from several builders before placing the contract. On a big project it is as well to commission an architect or surveyor to design the extension for you and supervise the actual building.

4 Visually, two factors can make or mar any extension or alteration to the exterior of your home: positioning and the materials chosen. Positioning of the extension and its relationship to the rest of the house can improve, or ruin, the proportions of your home. A perfect match in materials is difficult to achieve, especially in the case of old buildings. Failing this, a deliberate contrast is usually preferable to a near miss.

5 Plumbing. As a general rule, it is cheapest and easiest to extend the existing plumbing in a straight line for as short a distance as necessary. Putting in new plumbing is a specialist job which can be expensive. So consult an expert before planning a new bathroom, kitchen or utility room that is located some way from the existing plumbing and drainage systems.

6 Lighting. Here the problem is not so much where to put the new circuit as the practical matter of installing it. This should only be done by a qualified electrical engineer.

7 Heating. Your new extension is bound to require some form of heating. If you already have central heating, it may be possible to extend this without overloading the system. Otherwise you will need an auxiliary system or some form of spot heating.

8 The cost of extending your home is not just the building, decorating and furnishing expense involved. Extra rooms cost extra money as well as time to maintain. So take this into account when working out your budget, or you may find that your extended home, much improved though it is, strains domestic finances.

ADDED ON: ROOMS WITH A VIEW

How a bigger and better home came to be achieved by means of an extension that gives priority to upper floor living

To make the most of the fine view, the extension to the actual living area of this house has been concentrated at first floor level behind the old part of the house, as shown by the plan on the facing page. The new and spacious living area encompasses the main bedroom, which can be completely screened by sliding doors. Beneath the extension, two doors lead to a boiler house and a sauna bath.

The new living room and its adjoining bedroom are 45 ft. (13.7 m) long, carried on brick piers, with softwood beams and joists. As can be seen from the exterior photograph, there is an enormous area of window to make the most of the view. This is double glazed against noise and draughts. And the floor and roof of the extension have been strongly insulated. Double glazing and insulation add to costs. But in an extension they pay dividends in making the extra living space warmer and quieter, and they save money on heating bills.

Sliding doors play a useful role in a large open-plan extension. Here they cut off the bedroom at night but fold neatly back against the wall to leave the whole living area free for entertaining.

Access to the old part of the house is through what was once the window of the original living room (on the left in the picture of the interior).

Building on this extension involved the architect, June Park, in a general re-arrangement of the house. Now the upper floor is the main floor, enjoy-

the best views. As well as the new living room/bedroom, there are the old living room and dining area (seen on the left in the interior picture), another bedroom and a dressing room, a bathroom and a kitchen. Downstairs there is a garage, the sitting-out area (under the new extension) and the boiler room and sauna bath.

Without disturbing the original construction of the house — save for knocking out the wall in the old living room to link it with the extension — the house has been considerably enlarged and beautified.

The long living room and bedroom in the extension are lined with afrormosia planks, which are both decorative and have high insulating properties. The window frames are made of hard-

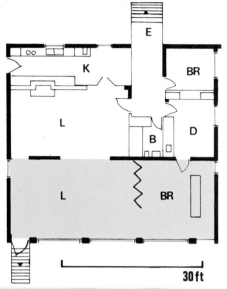

wood. See-through external nylon blinds in dark green shield the room from the hot sun in summer. The large windows frame the view by day. Full-length curtains give the room focal interest when drawn at night. The decor suits the nature of the room: the same materials on the floor and ceiling are used through the living and sleeping areas to link the two.

What was a not very exceptional house has become a much bigger and better home. And the extension will more than have paid for itself should the owner decide to sell the house.

On facing page: interior of new living/bedroom. This is heated by warm air through floor ducts.
Below: Extension seen from garden

COVERED WAY LINKS OLD AND NEW ②

Over the years, the water mill has been variously adapted as a home. Now old outbuildings have become a studio and garage, linked under cover with the main part of the house

This country property has existed for centuries, first as a water mill, later as a dwelling. The original mill still stands, but it has been added to progressively over the years by successive owners to take shape as a home.

When the present owners took over the mill, they decided that they needed more leisure room to suit the family's diverse interests. This meant major alterations and additions.

Designer Norman Westwater, who undertook the task, decided to utilize and add to existing outbuildings, which stood a little apart from the house, rather than attempt to modify the house itself. The group of outbuildings was L-shaped. He designed a garage to fit on the side facing the house, and a large studio to add on to the end of the outbuilding nearest the house, the latter linked with the house by a covered way, incorporating a new, generous entrance hall.

The studio, which has huge mullioned windows and a first floor gallery, provides the family with space for painting, film shows, photographic work — it has a dark room partitioned off — and general entertaining. The gallery provides office space at one end of the studio, and runs along two other sides. The studio opens into the covered way.

Including the new hall, the covered way is 45 ft. long, 18 ft. wide (13.7 m. x 5.5 m.), it has sliding glazed doors on the south side which can be closed for protection from wind and rain. The roof rests on oak columns. The floor is paved. This paving extends into the new entrance hall, and has been repeated in an ample hearth and step in the living room of the house to continue the link between old and new. The new hall contains a cupboard for coats and a lobby with a lavatory and basin, and more coat hanging space.

As a result of these brilliantly

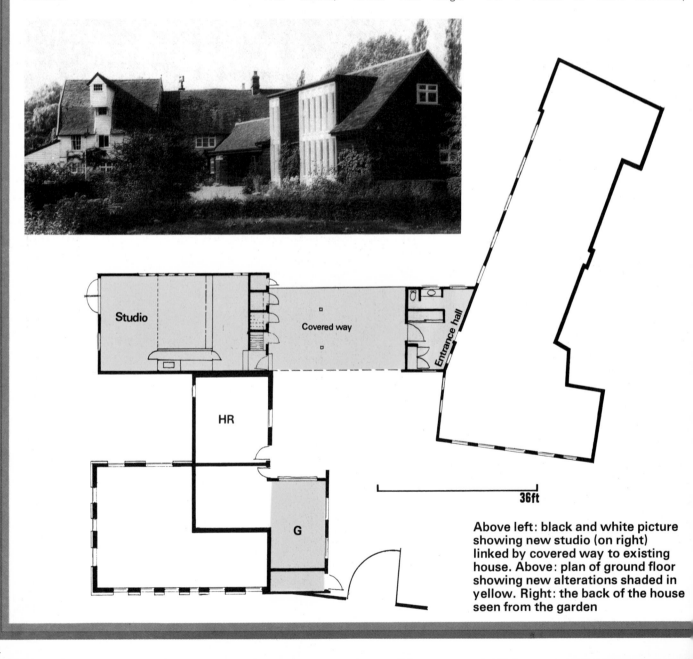

36ft

Above left: black and white picture showing new studio (on right) linked by covered way to existing house. Above: plan of ground floor showing new alterations shaded in yellow. Right: the back of the house seen from the garden

5

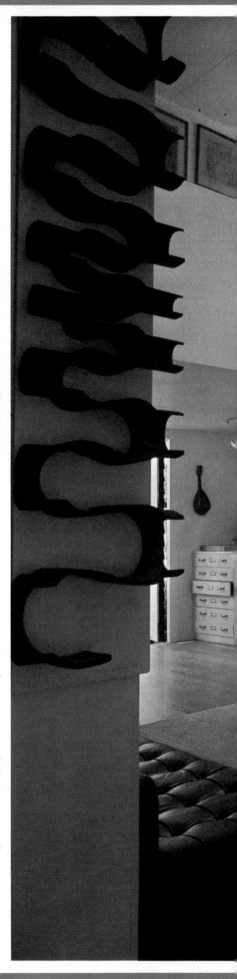

COVERED WAY LINKS OLD AND NEW ②

Above: the new studio connects with the covered way. Right: a gallery runs round three walls of the studio; decor is simple

designed additions, the external appearance of the house is much improved through the blending of the separate outbuildings with the house. Moving the entrance to the side has, in turn, greatly improved the approach to the house. Originally, a straight drive led from the front gate to an exposed area between the house and the outbuildings. Now, the new driveway sweeps from the main road in a curve around the outbuildings and studio to the edge of the weir, giving visitors ample opportunity to savour the beauty of the mill and its surroundings before disembarking in a courtyard encircled by the house, covered way, studio, original outbuilding and garage.

One of the designer's main concerns in this enterprise was to maintain the harmony of materials and design that had always been a feature of the mill during its evolution into a home. Thus,

the new studio and entrance hall are timber, faced with black weatherboarding. The outbuildings and the new garage are also clad with weatherboarding. Old roof tiles were obtained for the covered way and garage to blend with their fellows. The only striking 20th-century note on the exterior are the two walls of windows in the studio. These reach from the top of the new roof extension right down to the ground in twin sweeps, flooding the studio interior with daylight and, from the outside, giving this addition to the house a prominence that balances the unusual exterior of the mill section at the far end of the building.

Inside, the studio is very simply decorated. It is painted white all over — which both bounces back the daylight and makes a good background to hang hundreds of paintings. The mullioned windows have ventilation panels.

OFF-THE -PEG EXTENSION

Pre-fabricated home extensions are available as simple sun lounges or as a more complex series of rooms – as here

This pre-fabricated annexe extends an 'average' suburban two-storey house. The exterior makes no pretence at blending with the parent house; in fact, the owners set out to achieve a deliberate contrast.

The annexe juts out from the back of the house into a large terraced garden, and comprises a music room, dining room and an open-plan kitchen. A corridor separates it from the formal sitting room in the main part of the house itself.

Decor of the new rooms, although simple, is of a high standard in keeping with the rest of the house.

The furniture is light to match the mood of the annexe. The curtaining in the new living rooms (see the picture below) is wall-to-wall – necessary with so much window space and useful for keeping the room warm in winter.

③ See on this page, below left, an interior view of the music room. On facing page: the extension from the garden, looking into the music room. And a plan of the new extension, showing the rooms in relation to one another

The owners chose the particular type of extension partly because of the amount of uncluttered window space provided. Most ranges of pre-fabricated extensions offer a choice of different door and window fittings, and a choice of roofing types and exterior finishes. The selection is wide enough to cater for most people's tastes.

As with an architect-designed and builder-built extension, these units need proper sub-floors (such as a hard-core base beneath concrete or paving, fitted with a damp-proofing course). But there the similarity between the two types of extension ends. Since all the building materials are dry and ready cut to measure, construction is comparatively quick and clean. Some pre-fabricated units are available with suspended timber floors and foundation units. This dispenses with the chore of making a sub-floor. Provision is made for guttering (concealed or open, according to the purchaser's preference); and a wiring duct for electricity is supplied.

With most pre-fabricated models, the components in any wall can be inter-changed so that doors and windows can be positioned to suit the owner.

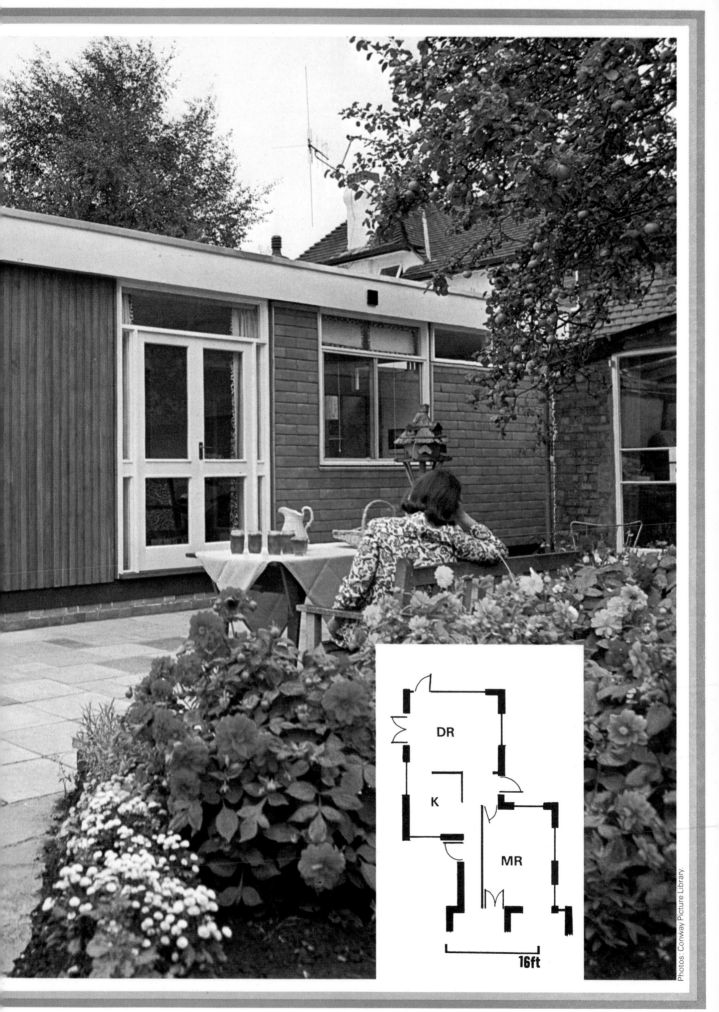

DR

K

MR

16ft

GARDEN ROOM WITH A SOUTHERN LOOK

Through the welcoming archway the additional room is well worth the terrace space it was built upon

This room that was added is perfectly positioned to catch the sun; it faces south and west. To build it, it was necessary to encroach upon the terrace but the owners felt that the result — an enclosed patio with a Mediterranean atmosphere — was worth the loss to the garden.

Classical arches, as used here for the windows and French windows, have a softening effect as opposed to the purely functional impression given by square or oblong windows. But they do tend to be more expensive. These were purpose-made, designed with small glass panes inside metal glazing bars.

To echo the window shapes an arch has also been used as the link between the dining room and sun room. And the two rooms follow the same basic colour scheme of blue and white. In open-plan decor, it is always better to link the two areas visually in one way or another rather than introduce an abrupt change of mood. Note the unusual ceiling of the extension. The beams are set lengthwise to give an impression of depth, and are picked out in white against a blue background that seems a harbinger of summer skies.

Across the far corners of the room, built-in cupboards break the right angles where the walls meet, and are lit to display white pottery against a blue background matching the ceiling.

Lacy, wrought-iron furniture matches the airy feeling of this room, while plants growing in different-sized pots make a link with the garden beyond. A white tiled floor gives a cool appearance and is easy to wipe clean, and white walls show off the shape of the arches to advantage.

From the outside, the extension blends well with the simple lines of the house. It has a flat roof, with short sloping sides immediately below this, hanging baskets full of flowers have been set between the window arches.

Drawing shows outside view of new sun lounge. Note how sloping sides to new roof echo feeling of roof of existing house above

GARAGE INTO LIVING ROOM

5

Here is an example of how to make a garage cosily fit for human habitation, easing the pressure on living space elsewhere in the house

The integral garage of this house was at garden level on one side of the house. It was as dismal as most garages, although it had the great advantage of a window looking on to the garden.

With a few basic precautions to fend off damp and to create more light, the scene was set for a dramatic transformation and the owners have gained – without structural additions – a comfortable, sunny living room with a garden view.

The concrete floor of the garage was sound and dry, but cold. It formed a good sub-structure for a vinyl tile floor, stuck down with a bitumen-based compound – a good means of keeping damp at bay. The walls were partly lined with softwood structural plywood panelling and the mean little window replaced with a wall of glass, making the most of the view over the garden. Wooden-framed folding shutters taking up the whole of the window wall make a decorative feature. Closed at night they give cosiness. During the day, they can be folded back on themselves.

A false ceiling was built to hide the trap door in the garage and to provide extra insulation. Use was made of an existing flue to install a neat free-standing fireplace whose tall chimney radiates warmth throughout the room.

The room was now transformed and merely awaiting furniture to assume whatever role the owners wanted it to fill. In fact, it has become an ancillary sitting and dining room. It would be ideal for use by teenagers entertaining their friends. Equally it could become a bed-sitting room.

Irrespective of its precise role as extra living space, the former garage follows the cardinal rules for low level conversion: treat or avert damp; provide light and warmth.

Where does the car go now? The owners have built a car port on to the side of the house.

Right: the warm and sunny-looking new living room created from the dismal garage shown below

13

Above: back of the house seen from the garden. Theo Crosby's studio is in the foreground; glass door leads to the dining area in the main part of the house. On the first floor, over the dining area, is a bedroom; over this, the second studio with its roof garden. Below: a plan of the ground floor of the house as it is today. On facing page, top picture shows a view of the house from the road in the first stage of its extension, with a new living room on the first floor to the left. Colour picture shows same view of house after Ann Crosby's studio had been built on (top right of picture)

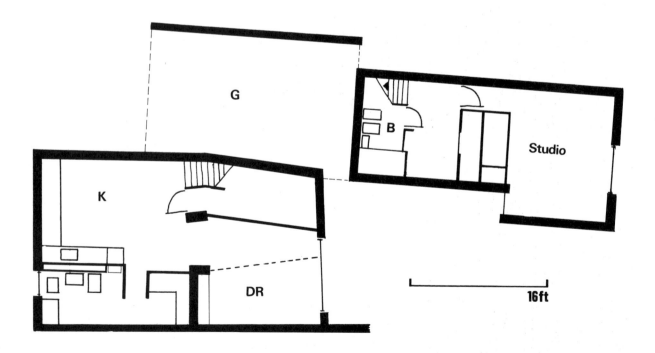

G

B

Studio

K

DR

16ft

Photos: Jessica Strang, Sam Lambert

If you can find a site with potential for development, there is no limit to the possibilities of extension. You see here how the architect owner of the spectacular house pictured used a stable and coach shed as the basis for his striking stage-by-stage improvements

When architect Theo Crosby found his home, it consisted of a stable and coach shed, with a loft above for storing food for the horses. It was quite uninhabitable as it stood, but full of possibilities — and sharing a long, wild garden behind.

Over the years, the original ramshackle building has been used as a basis for a number of additions until now it is a three-bedroom house, with two artists' studios and lots of living space. However, the quality of the original building has not been lost, since the owner-architect has been careful to retain a memory of the original by using similar materials and forms.

The first task was to make the stable into a habitable dwelling. Into the ground floor were fitted a kitchen, bathroom, living/dining room and a spiral staircase leading to a tiny bedroom in the loft, which was to be the temporary principal bedroom. Proper foundations were sunk and supporting pillars put in. New floors were laid throughout. The roof was relined, although the original tiles were retained — and two walls that collapsed during the alterations were replaced.

Since this first conversion, the house has virtually trebled in size, shooting both upwards and outwards in a series of controlled jumps. Today, at ground floor level, the kitchen is still where it was first sited and the coach shed/studio has become a proper dining room. A complete new section has been built on to adjoin the original building. This consists of a garage, a bathroom/shower, plenty of cupboards and a sculpture studio for the owner at the far end. The studio has a higher ceiling than the rest of this wing, with big windows cut in the roof for maximum light.

At first floor level, where there was

UPWARDS AND OUTWARDS

6 once a small bedroom there are now three bedrooms and a bathroom (built above the original stable). Plus a new, spacious living room, built on to the side of the house, supported by pillars, over a cobbled area that forms a car port. There are stairs leading down into the studio wing.

At second (or top) floor level, there is another studio for the owner's wife. From the exterior this looks like a chunky, square tower; it takes up half of the roof area, the other half being converted to a charming roof garden. Sliding glass doors in the studio link with this.

Achieving the spectacular house that you see on these pages took four stages of designing and building, each involving major structural alterations.

But this is the advantage of buying a building with potential; you can add to it as and when it suits your mood and pocket. And, if you wish, you can retain the flavour of the original dwelling as a basis to work around. Theo Crosby's house is a classic example.

On facing page in colour: a view of the new living room. This was one of the earlier additions to the house. It is built at first floor level, supported by pillars under one side and by the original section of the house under the other. On this page in colour (above): another view of the living room, showing the bedroom section and the stairs which lead to the new studio beyond. On facing page in black and white: the first alteration to the stables was to put in the kitchen equipment and plumbing shown here, and the spiral staircase. On this page in colour (left): a view of the dining room as it is now — looking through to the kitchen area beyond

INTO THE ATTIC: AN ENTIRE APARTMENT

7 Here is proof that living, eating and sleeping in an attic can be as luxurious as having a penthouse

This is the home of a French architect. It comprises a bedroom, living room/dining room, kitchen and bathroom. And it has been ingeniously converted from an attic measuring approximately 50 ft. by 21 ft. (15 m. by 6.4 m.).

It takes a second look at the picture below to realize that every millimetre of space has been used rationally to make a well-knit whole that yet divides into various areas.

Basically open plan, the bedroom is screened from the sitting area by the fireplace on a raised hearth. At the other end of the room the return wall in whitewashed brick makes a natural semi-partition for the dining room. The centre of the room houses the sitting area, with two settees along one long wall and the small but beautifully fitted kitchen across the room. A breakfast bar acts as a room divider between kitchen and living area, but folding doors make it possible to screen off the kitchen completely.

The walls throughout are white to

reflect the maximum light; either white-washed brick or pine boarding painted white. Light pours in from five large skylight windows and more light is reflected from the false ceiling in the middle of the living area, made out of copper sheeting. This false ceiling also helps to provide insulation, an important problem in an attic, partly solved by using a layer of fibreglass under the pine cladding on the rest of the ceiling.

Built-in shelves make the most of the shape of the walls and provide focal points with displays of books and ornaments. Storage furniture is built in, and the rest of the furniture is kept low, in keeping with the varying height of the room.

The colour scheme is simple. An off-white carpet covers the whole of the floor area and pale beige and brown and white skin rugs are dotted for comfort around the living room. The fitted orange covers on the settees are the only bright colour note. Warm brown armchairs and a medley of cushions complete the furnishing of the living area.

This comfortable, sophisticated flat provides an object lesson in deploying an attic to its limits. The open plan has made the most of the space. The white paint on walls and ceiling and on the struts supporting the roof minimizes the architectural bones of the house and makes the room look brighter. Plenty of windows, simply cut into the roof, seem to bring the sky into the room.

Where there isn't the space to build on to a house and the roof structure is suitable, using the attic can be a rewarding way of extending a house.

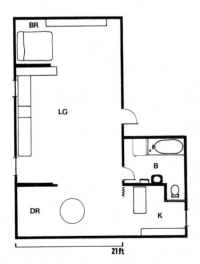

Left: the living area of the attic showing the fireplace which screens the bedroom. Top right: the bedroom. Below right: the neat, fitted kitchen

Photos: Transworld/Michael Gardett

MODERN BONUS FOR OLD HOUSE 8

This two-storey extension has added an L-shaped sitting room downstairs and a principal bedroom suite upstairs

It was an old stone house with a charming facade and great character. But the whole of the interior was in a state of decrepitude when the present owners decided to buy it. So their first job was to replace worm-eaten stairs and floorboards, strip damp plaster and to install a modern kitchen, a bathroom and gas central heating.

This left them with a comfortable home comprising a sitting room, dining room and kitchen downstairs and, upstairs, two fair-sized bedrooms, a tiny bedroom and a bathroom.

The accommodation, however, was not enough for their needs and so stage two was planned — the addition of a modern two-storey extension measuring 22 ft. by 12 ft. (6.7 m. by 3.7 m.). Upstairs they added a new principal bedroom suite, including a shower, WC and walk-in clothes cupboards, and turned one of the former bedrooms into a study. Downstairs they introduced a split-level addition to the sitting room, creating an L-shaped room with a total floor area of about 430 sq. ft. (39.9 sq. m.).

Three steps lead down to the old part of the sitting room. The new part has sliding floor-to-ceiling windows that front a small paved terrace outside, giving a lovely view of the garden. Thermal insulation in the new wing is provided by polystyrene foam in cavity walls and above the bedroom ceiling. There is also double glazing.

The decoration is part of the charm of the new wing. The walls are partly white and partly a warm sand colour to provide a good background for the display wall which has pictures, books and ornaments on a shelving system. A creamy carpet and beige and white settees are an effective foil for the rich orange curtains and make for a relaxed room, with furniture and lines so simple that it blends inconspicuously with the older part of the house.

A smaller extension on the ground floor only at the other end of the house has added a porch that not only provides shelter but contains a cloakroom, a washing machine and a useful toy cupboard for the children.

Two interior views of the extended living room (at left and above). Below: yellow portions on the plan show extensions

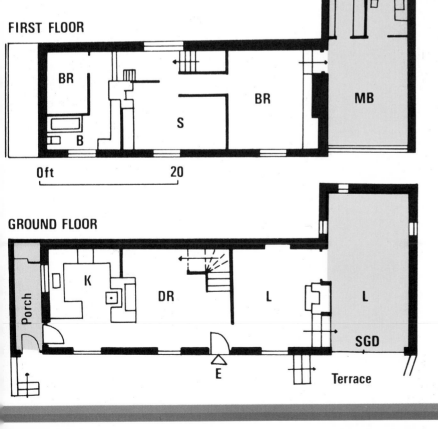

FIRST FLOOR

BR

BR

MB

S

B

0 ft   20

GROUND FLOOR

Porch

K

DR

L

L

SGD

E

Terrace

ALL-IN COMFORT BELOW GROUND LEVEL

⑨ A dull room in a cellar has been turned into a charming self-contained open-plan flat

What used to be office accommodation in a cellar has become a glossy flat for two, with a large dining table and simple cooking arrangements neatly built into a pine fitment at one end of the room.

The whole flat is contained in just one big room. Living, dining, cooking and sleeping areas are open-plan and take up over two-thirds of the total area. The bathroom is partitioned off at one end of the room, facing a wall of fitted clothes cupboards that include a dressing table unit.

The floors were sanded and sealed, and only a simple brown rug at the sitting end covers the wide expanse of warm wood. Walls and ceilings are painted white.

Cleverly thought-out built-in furniture includes a cupboard fitment in sealed wood built around the chimney breast (the chimney itself having been removed) to house the cooking facili-

Photos: Jessica Strang

ties and crockery and equipment. There is a wall-mounted grill and rotisserie, and a wipe-clean worktop. The bed fitment, also built-in, has drawers for storing linen in the base and a shelf at one end. An alcove in the wall at the head of the bed holds books and a reading lamp. A plain fitted brown cover gives the bed a suitably stream-lined look in this sophisticated room.

The very long dining table would take 12 people comfortably. A bench fitment runs on two sides of the wall near the table and four simple black chairs provide extra seating. The sitting end of the room has a handsome Chesterfield covered in black leather, and a pair of large brown leather stools and a pedestal chair. A pair of uncom-promisingly simple white coffee tables and a small white table by the bed complete the furnishings.

This is a room that would provide an excellent city *pied-à-terre* for a couple whose main home was in the country.

Above left: overall view of the multi-purpose room with the dining table on the right and sitting area on the left. Above: the bed fits next to the built-in fitment that houses the cooking equipment

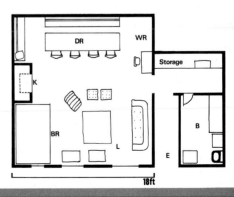

ADDITION TO A SUBURBAN HOUSE 10

A study and living room, with picture windows and a covered patio in between, have been added to the back of this house. What was the living room has become a dining room; the former dining room and study are now a guest room

Upstairs, nothing has changed. Downstairs, by building out two rooms and making use of the gap created between them, the living area of this surburban house has been greatly enlarged.

The exterior picture at left shows the rear of the house since it was extended. To the left is the new living room — 19 ft. 6 in. long and 13 ft. 9 in. wide (5.9 m. by 4.2 m.). Next to this is a covered patio, which is in turn adjacent to the other new room that has been added — a study, 13 ft. 9 in. by 10 ft. (4.2 m. by 3 m.). The finishing touch is the ornamental pool in front of the new living room, which was planned at the same time as the other alterations.

The motive for building on two rooms was, as for most extensions, to procure more space in a home that was becoming over-crowded. The obvious place to choose to build on was at the back because there was room to spare here by projecting into the garden, large enough for the purpose.

Now for the architects, John and Sylvia Reed, came the question of which room to put where. Building out the new living room on the extreme left, backing on to the garage, gave it a desirably southerly aspect. Making it long enough to suit its role meant extending the line of the house by some 10 ft. (3 m.) into the garden, and creating a semi L-shape at the back of the house. In view of this, the best position for the proposed study was at the opposite flank of the house. It too projects into the garden some 10 ft. (3 m.). Thus the projections of both rooms are in balance.

This extension in the form of two arms produced a sun-trapping gap between them. Part of this area has been cobbled to form a small inner courtyard. The remainder, which abuts

25

ADDITION TO A SUBURBAN HOUSE 10

the garden and lies between the new study and the new living room, has been roofed with 9 in. by 2 in. (229 mm. by 51 mm.) painted joists, and paved with slabs to form a terrace.

The new living room has a door giving on to the paved terrace. It has a complete glass wall overlooking the garden and the pool. A special feature of this room is the wine cellar, sunk under the outside corner of the room and accessible through a trap door cut in the wood floor.

When the study was built, storage space at the extremity of the house was provided for fuel and dustbins.

What was originally the dining area and study is now a guest bedroom. A partition wall that divided it into two was knocked through, and the posi-

tions of doors and windows adjusted to suit the revised lay-out of the house. From the new study, access to the rest of the house is through the guest bedroom. An external door from the study leads on to the new paved terrace.

Floor construction for the new rooms is the same in the study and living room: 1 in. panga-panga on 2 in. lightweight screed on a damp-proofing course, over 6 in. concrete slab and 6 in. hardcore. The flat roofs on both sides of the extension are made from granite chips on 3 in. ply bituminous felt, on 2 in. stramit slabs, on 9 in. by 2 in. softwood joists, on $\frac{1}{2}$ in. plaster board, on $\frac{3}{4}$ in. pine boarding. The flashing is aluminium; the gutters plastic. The walls are solid brick beneath the level of the damp-proofing

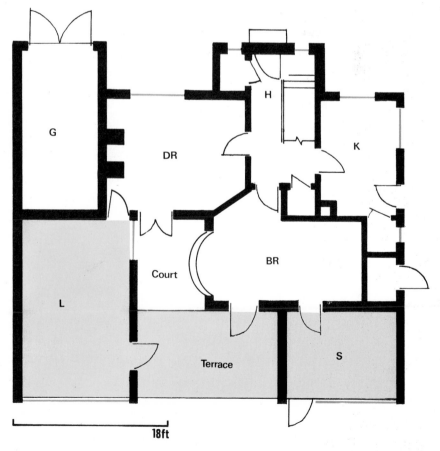

course; above it come 3 in. breeze inner leaf and 4½ in. brick outer leaf with a 2 in. cavity.

Built-in electric skirting heaters provide warmth in winter, which the wood ceilings in both rooms help to retain. Interior decor is in tune with the rest of the house, although the owners took the opportunity of sinking spotlights into the new ceilings as they were put in.

Above: the new living room, with a picture window overlooking the ornamental pool. Above right: the study was built out to balance the living room. Right: plan of the ground floor of the house. The additions are shaded yellow

TOPPED BY A STUDIO ROOM 11

This colourful room used to be the unused loft of a one-storey villa. The extension upwards proved simple and inexpensive, the owners doing most of the work themselves

Both ends of the roof of this house consisted of vertical gable walls and there were no supporting beams across the main loft space; the roof weight is supported on two main beams, strengthened by brick pillars running along each side of the loft. On the debit side, there were no windows and no floor — just the exposed ceiling joists.

The first step was to create a source of daylight. A skylight window was cut by removing 12 of the roof tiles and supporting battens, but the roof rafter was left to run down the centre of the new window.

Insulation was the next thing to be tackled. The roof space between the rafters was insulated with kitchen foil stapled on to fibreboard and fixed to the roof with battens. The floor was insulated with glass fibre between the joists and the floor boards were laid on top of this. The walls under the slope of the roof were made of chipboard on a timber frame, fixed to a main horizontal beam that supports the roof.

Stage three was to move the water tank from its position near the trap-door to the loft to an unobtrusive corner. This left an uninterrupted floor area of some 24 ft. by 15 ft. (7 m. by 4.6 m.).

Safe access is important in this kind of conversion. Here it is provided by a fixed ladder from the hall below into the trapdoor, which has been enlarged and surrounded on three sides by a 'cage' of four tiers of wooden rails. This is sealed on the loft side.

The beams have been left exposed as a decorative feature and the cable which brought electricity into the loft runs along the apex of the roof and has been painted to blend in with the beams. The rest of the decor is simple and striking. The end walls are painted red over the natural brickwork. The other walls and the space between the rafters are white. The wooden floor has been sanded and sealed.

Most of the furniture in this studio room in an attic is home-made, including the bright crochet rug and cushions. The rest was bought second-hand from sales. An inflatable plastic seat adds casual comfort to a room which has brought a new dimension to the small house underneath it and could well serve as a teenager's bed-sitter or as a guest room

Scarlet loft ladder links the studio room to the rest of the house

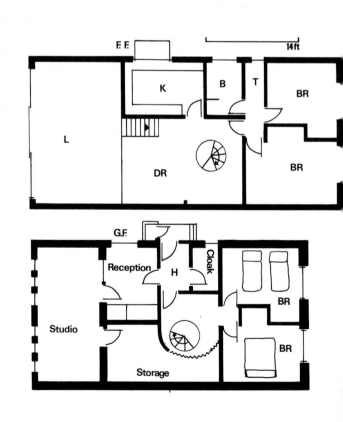

NEW FLOOR MAKES IT A HOME

A cantilevered top-storey has created a capacious riverside family home out of a single-storey structure that was once a bus station

A brick-built single-storey structure — it once served as a bus station — has been used imaginatively as the base of a second-storey extension.

The ground floor is more or less as it was, apart from minor alterations such as the re-positioning of windows. The two roof levels of the original structure have been exploited to create a two-level first floor living area. The ground floor now contains two bedrooms facing the road; an entrance hall and cloakroom, and a reception room opening into a studio that faces the river running past the property.

The new upper storey has been cantilevered forward on the river frontage. Apart from bringing the house nearer the river, this has increased the living space upstairs without affecting the ground floor structure. The upper extension comprises a living room facing the river, with a split-level dining room, a kitchen, a bathroom and W.C. and two bedrooms on the opposite side facing the road. For reasons of privacy, one side elevation of the upper storey is a blank wall, while the other side elevation contains only small windows for the kitchen, bathroom and W.C.

To meet fire regulations that had to be observed on such a narrow site, the top floor was built of insulating blocks clad with textured asbestos sheeting. The ground floor brickwork was painted with a black bituminous oil varnish. All the outside woodwork is white, and the result is an attractive finish plus the bonus that the paint on the bricks has hidden the junction between the old and the new.

The unusually designed bay windows at the front minimize noise.

Inside, the main feature of the house is the specially designed spiral staircase that leads the eye up to the main living area. The architect, Kenneth Wood, designed a roof lantern at the top of the staircase which lets in daylight during the day.

Warm wooden floors, fir-boarded ceilings and plain walls put the onus for impact on the river view, the great charm of this unusual house.

On facing page (top): a view of the front of the house since its conversion; see (immediately above) the same view of the house before conversion. On facing page (lower picture): the converted house seen from the river. Left: the plans of the house after conversion — top plan shows top floor. On this page (top picture): the living room is on the first floor so as to give the best view of the river. The stairs lead up to the living room from the ground floor

OPENING UP A KITCHEN

13

Before (below) and after (at right): what an improvement! Out went the pantries; in came streamlined units

The original kitchen in this rambling house forfeited working space because of two small dark pantries — one at each end — and suffered from a bad layout. Eliminating the pantries to add the space to the kitchen proper and redesigning the layout have improved the kitchen beyond recognition.

Instead of pantries, the kitchen now has streamlined units and cabinets built in around the walls. These provide more than enough storage space.

Although positioned as before, the two sets of windows have been greatly widened. To do this, it was necessary to reinforce the wall with a rolled steel joist in each case. Well worthwhile, since the room is now light and airy to work in.

Refrigerator, dishwasher, sink and cooker are built into an L-shaped arm of units, so that moving from one to the other involves minimum effort. A breakfast bar, with a hinged flap to enlarge it, adjoins the end of the arm.

The floor, which was in very poor condition when renovation of the kitchen began, has a plywood underlay to make a smooth base for the tiles. The ceiling has been lowered two feet (609 mm.) to make it a height of about eight feet (2.4 m.), and this takes all the new wiring, plumbing arrangements and heating system for the room.

Note in the picture at right the two lights lowered over the table. It is always a good idea to have direct light for eating. There are three double sockets for electrical gadgets strategically placed around the kitchen. A minimum of three points is essential in any kitchen and, if you are starting from scratch, double sockets cost very little more than single to install.

The kitchen as it was and (right) in its enlarged, restyled form

COTTAGE THAT'S GONE ON GROWING

14 A 'two up, two down' 17th century cottage is at the heart of this interesting conversion in several stages, which includes a large barn transported in numbered pieces from several miles away

The original cottage is still the centre of this home, with the kitchen and sitting room downstairs and the main bedroom and dressing area above. Around this, forming three sides of a rectangle and enclosing a delightful courtyard, are the additions designed by Derek Phillips. The first structure to be added, to the east at right angles to the cottage, comprised an entrance hall, bathroom and two guest rooms, all on one floor but with the same roof height as the cottage. The next stage was the addition of a studio, leading from the hall, for the artist owner. This studio has a door leading into the next addition — a conservatory, which is

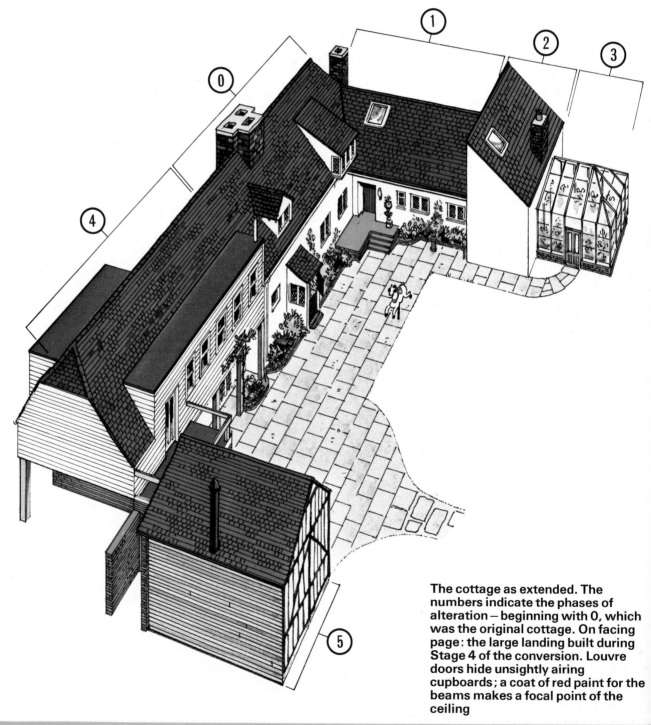

The cottage as extended. The numbers indicate the phases of alteration — beginning with 0, which was the original cottage. On facing page: the large landing built during Stage 4 of the conversion. Louvre doors hide unsightly airing cupboards; a coat of red paint for the beams makes a focal point of the ceiling

Don Kidman

used as a working greenhouse.

The largest addition is at the west end of the house. It is a two-storey continuation of the cottage, with three bedrooms, a large landing and a sun deck above a dining room, an entrance passage, garage and car port. The addition has been blended in with the exterior of the cottage by the use of old roof tiles which match those on the original cottage. The upper storey is clad in white-painted weather boarding, in keeping with local old houses.

Some of the materials inside the new wing are old, such as the quarry tiles used to floor the dining room; they combine happily with modern ameni-

ties like the underfloor heating in the dining room.

The final addition (or perhaps the latest, as there is no telling whether the owners feel that their home is even now complete!) is the most interesting. It is a large barn set at right angles to the new wing and brought in carefully numbered sections from a site several miles away. Heavily timbered and lofty, it has been left open on one side facing the courtyard to make a perfect setting for parties and barbecues. Apart from the cooking fire fitted with a spit, there is a large open fireplace which burns logs. Steps lead up to a gallery in the barn which, in

its turn, leads to the sun deck in the new wing, thus linking house and barn.

Enclosed by the house, the courtyard is charming, with flower beds and climbing plants. It leads into the garden, lined with graceful trees and containing unusual features such as a circle of tall stone columns from various demolition sites that now support trailing and climbing plants.

The whole house is a tribute to the owner's vision and long-term planning. So well knit is it that it is difficult to believe three centuries separate the original from the additions.

For a relatively small outlay, the owners of the house have extended downwards — clearing the cellar of its accumulated junk to create a wonderland for the children

Probably the biggest expense in extending down in this house to make a room for the children out of a junk cellar was the cork floor. Warm and tough, it deadens sound and is easy to clean.

A large cupboard was fitted into a corner of the cellar. A long shelf links it to a desk in the other corner. Above this are simple shelves.

The rest of the room is pure fun. There is a climbing frame along one wall with a slide hinged to the front. A rope ladder firmly secured to the ceiling spans the room and provides scope for exercise and endless games. On the wall facing the shelf fitment there is room for self-expression; in a sort of artist's corner, large rolls of paper hang rather like a roller blind. A marvellous idea! The child just pulls the paper down, draws and paints to his heart's content, then rips off the finished product and starts again on a new length of paper. Crayons, pencils, brushes and colouring materials are stored in bicycle baskets clipped on to a rod on the wall within easy reach of the child, yet out of the way.

This is a room where no child need ever be bored, where children can escape from a wet day — out of sight and mercifully out of earshot — to romp about without inconveniencing anyone else in the house.

Safety is an important point to observe in installing children's games. Swings and rope ladders must be firmly anchored to wall or ceiling with steel fittings. Climbing frames must be sturdy, well put together and without protruding nails or rough wood surfaces. The floor should not be hard; cork chosen for this cellar playroom is an ideal choice — resilient yet durable.

With children, heating and lighting are both potential danger zones. In this room, heating comes from a radiator half way up the wall and the ceiling lights provide good overall lighting without trailing flexes.

Above: the junk cellar in its original state. Left and below: now, a new playroom for the children, full of exciting opportunities

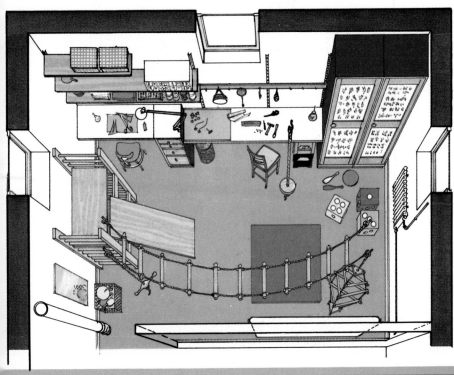

GLASS ROOM 16 GIVES EXTRA LIVING SPACE

Compatible plants and people can co-exist happily in a glass room. The one shown is a decorative extension to the living space of the house

A conservatory or glass room extension has a double advantage: it offers more leisure space, on the one hand, and fulfils a functional purpose housing and nurturing plants, on the other. Decor can be simple – the plants provide it!

However, before deciding to build a conservatory, it is advisable to clarify whether its main use is to be for plants or people, since some specimens do not mix! Jungle orchids, for example, require degrees of temperature that are unpleasant to humans and, if you intend cultivating that kind of plant, it will need the conservatory to itself. However, if you are content with less demanding plants, you could fill the greenhouse with the type of blossoms that enjoy the same micro-climate as people – heated in the winter and cooled in the summer.

The glass room shown here was purpose-built to fit on to the side of the house, and it opens from the drawing room to make a superb extra room. It is furnished with a table and chairs for light meals. Diamond-patterned rush matting is on the floor. Overhead, wooden blinds provide shade on particularly sunny days.

There are firms that specialize in making greenhouses either to fit the side of your house or to be free-standing. There are also models available in kit form for the handyman to put up himself. These are a good deal cheaper. Although – as with all extensions that are to be actually lived in – you must in most cases add on the cost of laying a solid concrete and hard-core base flooring.

Plan below shows the conservatory with glass on three sides added to the drawing room of the house

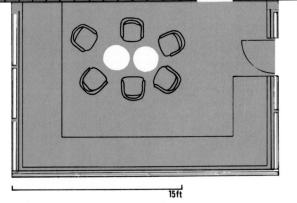

15 ft

Photos: Transworld

BUILT ON TO THE BACK PORCH 17

The house has gained a room. True the garden has lost some space. But it has won more privacy and a terrace for informal outdoor meals

This is a compact detached family house. But it suffered from a complaint common to many family homes: cramped conditions as the family grows and the children need more space — perhaps their own sitting room to entertain their friends — without robbing their parents of the use of the living room.

In this case the solution was obvious. Sacrifice a piece of the garden at the back of the house. Turn the back porch window into a door leading into a new room.

One step links the new room with the house. French windows lead out-

Right: the house showing the back porch before the extension was built on. Below: the new room and the enclosed terrace. Far right: the interior of the new room is warm and inviting

side to a newly constructed terrace with a wooden floor. Two windows give a view of the garden. And the bulk of the room screens the terrace from the house next door. There are no windows on the back wall of the room facing the next house.

Inside, the extension room is warm and inviting. The walls are faced with plywood. A wall of storage cupboards and shelves backs on to the porch There is a warm red carpet covering the whole floor. The roof girders have been left exposed and lighting is concealed behind them, transforming them into a decorative feature.

When there is the space to do so, building on to the back of a house is an ideal solution. It leaves the front of the house untouched. It does not disturb the façade and whatever contribution that makes to the overall look of the immediate neighbourhood.

If the addition makes an L-shaped house it will also create a small private sitting-out area that can be made very attractive with pot plants and climbers. This can be a big bonus in high density built-up areas where privacy is at a premium.

NEW ROOMS
BRIDGE TWO
COTTAGES   18

Having bought and renovated a charming country cottage some years ago, the owners were delighted when the neighbouring cottage came up for sale. They bought that, too, and bridged the gap between the two properties with a modern 'wing', carefully designed to blend with its traditional surroundings

The pretty pink cottage to the left of the picture shown here once stood on its own – some 13 ft. (4 m.) away from its neighbour. When the owners of the pink cottage were able to buy the one next door, they decided to link the two. The brief they gave to the architect, P. J. Aldington, was to design an addition that incorporated a living room, placed so as to enjoy as much afternoon and evening sun as possible, since this was something missing in their home as it stood.

The bridge between the cottages, as shown on these pages, consists of a living room, cloakroom and lavatory downstairs; and, above, a small gallery room used as a sewing-cum-work room, slung from the roof.

The architect found that to fulfil his brief and design a living room that caught the late sun, it was necessary to project into the garden well out beyond the existing line of the two cottages. There was already an outhouse facing the gap between the cottages, so he decided to link the new addition to this – thus retaining a degree of privacy in outlook for each cottage.

Downstairs, he put a cloakroom and lavatory on the front of the house, then the new living room, which stretches out into the garden to join the outhouse. It has sliding glass doors along one side wall to catch the sun, and a low, sloping tiled roof which follows the line of the existing cottages' roofs.

Internally, all the structural timbers are laid bare to form a modern counterpart to the exposed beams and frames in the two adjacent cottages. The walls are basically concrete blocks, which have been rendered to match the original walls of the cottages (made of

Photos: Brecht-Einzig

Plan of ground floor of the first cottage and the new 'wing' built on its side (to connect with second cottage). See in the picture below: left, the original cottage, which is pink with a thatched roof; next to it and projecting out into the garden is the new extension, housing a living room below and work room above, with picture windows; next to this, the second cottage (with only thatched roof visible)

NEW ROOMS BRIDGE TWO COTTAGES 18

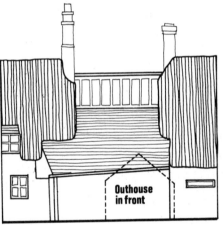

Outhouse
in front

Drawing shows elevation of extension from garden side. On facing page: interior of new living room where ceiling has been left deliberately bare to match old part of cottages. Above: wall of windows for new living room, carefully placed to catch late sun

the traditional local 'mud' and rendered). The windows are un-mistakably modern in concept, being large, single sheets of glass, but their form and chunky quality has been designed to respect and enhance the simple qualities of the cottages.

Externally, structural timbers in keeping with those on the existing cottages have been used. The walls are built from stone found on the site. The new roofs have been made from local tiles.

In the small sewing-cum-work room on top of the new addition, big picture windows 'front' the room while, inside, the roof slopes backwards, thus letting direct sunlight reach to the back of the room.

In view of their new-found space,

the owners have re-arranged the layout of their home. The original pink cottage now consists of a good-sized dining room, kitchen, hall (which was once the living room), and the additional new living room, cloakroom and toilet. The adjoining cottage has been re-windowed and re-orientated so that, as far as possible, the rooms face south. It now consists of two comfortable bedrooms and a bath-room.

Generally it is more difficult to achieve a successful addition to an old house, where there is a danger of new clashing with old.

However, bold use of modern materials in a style that complements the old has produced an entrancing result.

EXTENDING DOWN INTO THE CELLAR 19

Sitting room, bar, meals corner, hobby space; all contained in what used to be a barren cellar, now made cold-proof and damp-proof

Cold and damp are more often than not a problem in cellars.

Here, the concrete floor has been covered with sleepers of 1 by 4 in. (25 mm. by 102 mm.) plywood, applied by nails 'shot' into the concrete. Between the sleepers, sheets of foamed styrene have been stuck to the slab with a waterproof solution. This styrene has both cushioning and insulating properties, vital to a cellar floor. Glue was then spread over the styrene before laying $\frac{1}{2}$-in. (12.7 mm.) plywood. The result is a superb sub-floor, suitable for laying any kind of top floor.

The walls have also been insulated in this versatile additional living room—before finishing with an attractive wood panelling. Wood is an excellent decorating material for walls that are in a state of disrepair. It covers blemishes, keeps in warmth, looks attractive and lasts for a long time without needing any upkeep (provided it has been sealed initially).

The ceiling here is lined with stick-on acoustic tiles that deaden noise travelling upwards or downwards.

These three treatments for cellar floors, walls and ceilings are worth copying. So, too, is the general layout of this 24 ft. square (2.2 sq. m.) room, which is divided into four areas: a bar; a sitting out section; a meals corner and a place for sewing or hobbies, which can be screened off by wall-paper-covered plywood panels that slide on tracks.

Not everyone can have a real fireplace in the cellar, since the cost of putting in a chimney would be prohibitive. But it would be possible to emulate cheaply the effect of the one in the room shown (picture below) by using a plastic wallpaper designed to give a three-dimensional effect of stone in the background, building in a simple wood frame to flank the 'fire place' and fitting a free-standing electric heater into the frame.

On facing page: converted cellar seen from fireplace end. On this page: view of sitting area and bar corner on right of room

Photos: American Plywood Association

IT'S TWICE WHAT IT WAS 20

A single-storey villa with two bedrooms has burgeoned into a four-bedroom home with a linking extension added to the back of the original house

This small one-storey villa in a select residential neighbourhood was made up of two bedrooms, a dining room, living room, a small bathroom and a kitchen.

The owners wished to turn the original structure into a four-bedroom wing with a bathroom, and to build on a modern open plan unit incorporating a long living room and a dining room leading into a kitchen.

In order to make the most of the open garden view and to fit in with stringent local building regulations, the new structure was added to the back of the house and linked to it by an entrance lobby and a shower room unit.

The new wing is not visible at all from the road, and is designed to fit the rising ground at the back of the cottage. The mono pitch roof links with the tiled roof of the older property and the exterior of the new wing is in stained boarding and brickwork painted white to match the older house. There are large windows on all sides to make the most of the sun and the view of the garden.

Inside the extension, the ceiling, which follows the slope of the roof, is in sealed timber boarding and most of the walls are white-painted brickwork. Both the living room and the dining end have French windows opening on to a new terrace around the house. The interior of the original cottage was gutted and replanned completely to make four large bedrooms and a bathroom, all opening off a long passage leading directly into the lobby of the new extension.

The architect, Kenneth Wood, made no attempt to imitate the style of the cottage, which he felt was an entity in itself, and the new extension, uncompromisingly modern in its lines, is entirely successful. Only the areas of white brickwork in the new unit echo the materials of the older house, but this tenuous visual link is enough to bridge the gap in styles.

Photos: Architecture & Landscape Library

Left: the dining area of the new living room has a serving hatch through to the kitchen. Above: view of the exterior of the new wing; note how the architect has deliberately designed the new wing in a contrasting modern style. Yellow on the plan indicates extension

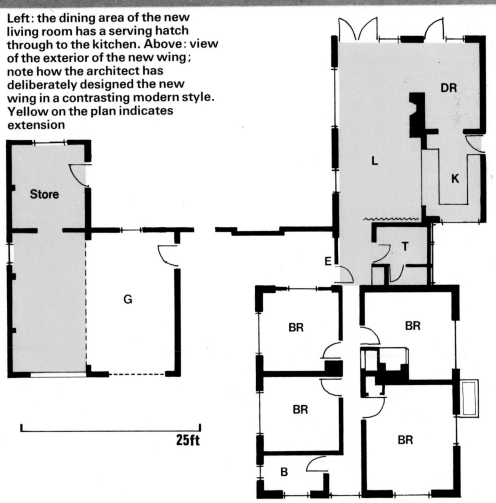

Store

G

DR

L

K

E

T

BR

BR

BR

BR

B

25ft

WHOLE NEW WING WAS ADDED 21

The extension to a pair of semi-detached country cottages uses traditional materials but in a modern style. It has given the owners a new hall, dining room, kitchen, two bedrooms, a sewing room, bathroom and — not least an elegant new staircase

The owners of this charming property were faced with an all-too common problem: that of having found an old place of considerable character in the right area but with the in-built disadvantages of many old dwellings — not enough space and very small rooms (even after, as in this case, two semi-detached cottages had been merged into one).

The answer was to extend the semi-detached cottages. The architect, Roger Worboys, faced with the choice of trying to imitate the old or build a totally modern addition, opted for an interesting compromise. He has used traditional building materials that blend with the old façade, but he has used them in a modern idiom.

The new wing consists of a hall, a dining room and a kitchen downstairs plus a laundry room and a garage, car port and outhouses. Upstairs there are two bedrooms, a sewing room and a bathroom.

Linking the two floors is an elegant sweeping staircase (pictured on the following pages) which is the most exciting feature in the new wing. To make the most of it, the staircase hall with a double height window is separated from the dining room by a sliding door, so that when this is slid out of sight and the glass doors on to the terrace are open there is a continuous view through to the garden — totally different in feeling and conception of space from the cosy low-ceilinged sitting room in the old part of the house.

Here too there were changes. Part of the ground floor of the cottages was opened up to make a large sitting room with exposed beams and an inglenook fireplace. Off this there is a smaller room with a large fireplace. The room tends to be used as a retreat when the family are alone on winter evenings. The old staircase leads to the top floor and three bedrooms and two

Photos: Sam Lambert

WHOLE NEW WING WAS ADDED

bathrooms, which can also be reached by the new staircase in the extension.

So, inside the extended home, the mood between old and new is deliberately different and clearly defined. Outside, despite the change in building styles, the two ends of the house blend surprisingly well. This is partly achieved because the roof lines blend and because old tiles have been used on the new roof to match the old. The bricks of the new wing blend with the mellowed bricks of the old house and, in between, the large modern windows set in a natural wood framework look perfectly at home. Window boxes spilling summer flowers soften the line and seem to merge the house with the charming garden it overlooks.

Already creepers are growing on the walls of the extended house, giving the look of an established and well-loved family home.

On facing page: an interior view of the new wing, showing the elegant curving staircase which links ground and first floors. Below, plans of the ground and first floors as converted.

PATIO BRINGS LIGHT AND CHARM 22

It replaces a small glazed veranda with a dreary view of an old wall and now provides a charming private spot for informal meals

Better light and a better view were imperative in this old suburban house, where the once dismal semi-basement had to house a new dining room and a new kitchen.

It was decided to have the dining room on the garden side and, as the floor level was considerably below the garden, the existing veranda was removed, the ground excavated and a patio built with a new retaining wall about 12 ft. (3.7 m.) away from the house. A large window was made in the dining room wall with French doors leading to the patio, a double steel joist having been inserted over the window opening to strengthen the brickwork.

The patio has been floored with old slabs and tiles which came from a barn. The walls around it have been colour-washed to reflect light and provide a good contrast for climbing plants. A metal staircase has been erected to provide access to the garden from the patio and a matching metal balustrade encloses the patio for safety. There is even room on the new patio for a lean-to greenhouse where the owners grow house plants.

The dining room itself was completely revamped, with a hardwood floor laid upon waterproofed basement slab. The room has electric underfloor heating. Next to it now is a well planned kitchen with pine cupboards. A new window and a glazed door let in as much light as possible.

The improvement to the back of the house is sensational. Although the garden has lost a few feet, the gain to the house in terms of comfort and improved proportions more than compensates. And, in a terrace house, the patio gives more privacy for sitting out than the garden.

Left and below: the back of the house before alteration. Above and on facing page: the new dining room seen from inside and out

A ROOM TRANSFORMED 23

Re-arrangement of furniture and some simple carpentry have given what was a rather ordinary double bedroom an attractive wider role

Space was at a premium in this small apartment, where a young married couple live with their two children. There was no way of extending the dimensions of the apartment, yet the family desperately needed an auxiliary living room . . . somewhere to work or sew while others watched television or entertained friends. The solution lay in a face-lift for the parents' bedroom, now radically re-arranged, which is seen in the picture below as it used to be and, on the facing page, as it now is.

The first step was to discard the tiny bedside tables in the room and to introduce twin beds, one along each of two walls. In these positions, they form comfortable sofas by day. A narrow wooden ledge has been built behind the beds along both walls to hold possessions, and give a tailored feel to the room. The beds sit upon painted wood frames which are hollow. These frames could usefully contain storage drawers.

The next step in the transformation was to board in the radiator running along the window wall with a deep shelf that now acts as a dressing table and holds adjustable reading lights.

To the end of one bed is appended a built-in writing table with a chair. The other bed end projects into a deep chest. Thick rolls of chunky foam, covered with linen that matches the bright bedspread and curtains, line the edges of the beds by day to turn them into sofas. A plastic 'pouch' screwed to the wall by the desk holds pencils, paper clips and odds and ends . . . yet another idea worth copying from this small room transformed so neatly from necessity.

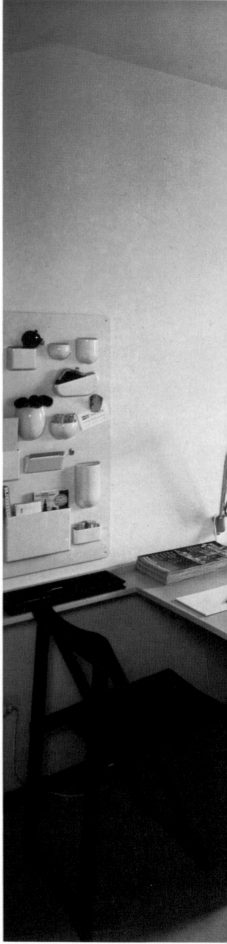

Below: this was how the room pictured in colour on the facing page looked before alteration. Note how much space has been saved by simple built-in furniture and re-arrangement of the beds

ADDING A SUN LOUNGE

24

The purpose of building on to this already large house was not to gain space, but to gain more sun. The sun lounge extension has three walls which are virtually all window

A southern outlook is best at trapping the sun, and such a vast area of glass as deployed in the sun lounge extension shown here magnifies whatever solar heat there is. Even in winter, just a small amount of sun will warm this room up very fast.

This custom-built extension was designed for the owners of the house by an architect, Peter Summersgill, and every detail is tailored to the site and their specific requirements. A cheaper way of achieving a sun lounge is to buy 'off the peg' (as shown elsewhere in this book). A pre-fabricated unit can be assembled at home by keen, strong amateurs.

The new sun lounge pictured here adjoins the sitting room of the house. It is a big room — stretching the full width of the house with an overlap of some 7 ft. (2 m.), totalling 24 ft. 7 in. (7.4 m.). This overlap wall is a pair of glass doors leading to a paved terrace immediately outside. The room is 14 ft. 10 in. (4.5 m.) deep.

One end of the room houses a dining-table and chairs for sunny meal-times; the other end (nearest the terrace) is furnished as a sitting room for relaxing. The west wall (facing the terrace) is fitted with full-height, full-width sliding glass panels which open. The other two exterior walls (south and east) have windows reaching from just under the flat roof to approximately 1½ ft. (457.2 mm.) from the ground.

Every alternate window is on a centre pivot for opening.

The exterior walls are cavity walls, painted white to match the brickwork of the existing house. Inside the room, a window sill runs round the south and east walls, with bookshelves built in between sill and floor levels.

Three roof lights, each 4 ft. square (37.2 sq.deci.) let in plenty of light during the day, and are fitted with concealed fluorescent tubes to give an impression of daylight in the evenings.

Heating for the winter is by thermostatically controlled electric convectors (fitted with time switches for economy), built into the internal walls. The floor has a 6 in. (152.4 mm.) hard-core base for site concrete, damp-proofing course and sub-floor. It is carpeted from wall to wall. The ceiling is finished with polystyrene tiles.

This de luxe sun lounge is an appendage that adds far more to the house in terms of comfort and enjoyment than it costs in money.

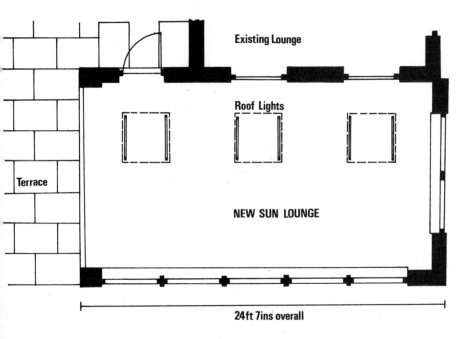

Existing Lounge

Roof Lights

Terrace

NEW SUN LOUNGE

24ft 7ins overall

Above and facing page: the new sun lounge added on the side. The white walls of the room match the white exterior of the existing house, and the big picture windows match the window of the adjacent living room. Left: a plan of the sun lounge

EXPANSION IN TWO STAGES 25

A sparse little house, in which a farmworker once lived, has blossomed into a dream home by means of an imaginative open-plan extension

One wall of the derelict brick house adjoined the road. So the first priority of the new owners was to turn the house away from the road. This was done by replacing the boundary hedge with a high brick wall that completely shut out the road. New windows were cut to make the most of the view and at a later date a two-room addition was built on.

The owners had to put in drainage, a bathroom and lavatory and have the roof repaired. They did much of the carpentry, decorating and making good themselves, employing a builder for the structural work on the roof, the plumbing and the fitting of new large windows, eight in all. It took a year of almost maniacal hard work to turn the house into a charming country home enhanced by personal furnishing touches.

With the birth of a baby and the chance to buy some adjoining land, the owners seized the opportunity to build on a studio for the husband, who is a photographer.

The architect, Roger Dyer, had no easy brief. The new extension had to suit the working requirements of a busy photographer as well as the living requirements of a family: it had to turn its back on the road and not obstruct the view from the bedroom, which the owners prized and had created by adding three windows to the room.

The outcome is an uncompromisingly modern addition that complements the old house beautifully. It has wall to wall sliding glass doors on two floors facing south over the garden. There are three small bedrooms and a large playroom on the ground floor and, above, a large studio.

The view from the main bedroom has been preserved, for the bedroom, with a balcony, is now the link between the old house and the new. Below it is an enclosed raised terrace.

During the day the extension is filled with sun and light. At night, when lit up, it seems to give back to the night outside the warmth and light absorbed during the day.

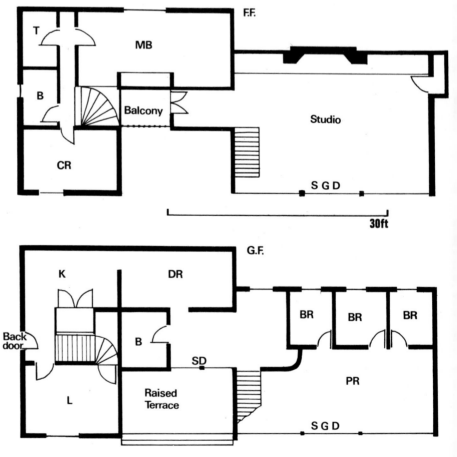

Above: the original house. Right: plans show the extension – the studio on the first floor with three bedrooms and the playroom below. Facing page, top: the house at night; below: the new studio leading down to the playroom

Photos : Michael Boys

EXTENSIONS: A GLOSSARY

What you need to know technically if
you plan to extend your home

Foundations are solid supports sunk low enough into the ground to take the weight of the building over them. There are basically two types: strip and raft. The right type for your extension depends on the kind of soil and on the weight of the building the foundations will have to sustain.

If you are leaning a new building against the side of an existing house, take an expert's advice as to whether the foundations beneath the existing connecting wall need underpinning (digging holes beneath the existing foundations and adding to them). This can be expensive, but is better than the new room sinking!

Every extension needs some kind of foundation.

Flooring depends to a certain extent on the type of building you are going to put up. A typical heavyweight sub-floor consists of six inches (152 mm.) of hardcore base; then four inches (102 mm.) of concrete slab; a damp-proof membrane; and a two-inch (51 mm.) concrete screed lining. This type of floor suits most buildings. An alternative — but only feasible where the framework of the new building is pretty solid — is a suspended timber floor on joists, with air-space left beneath.

External walls should be built with a cavity to stop damp penetrating, and should also be fitted with a damp-proof course. External brick walls which are very exposed to the weather should be sealed with a special patent water-proofing liquid. Or rendered with a coat of cement mortar. Or clad with tiles; sheeting set on battens; or overlapping timber boards.

For added insulation, the cavity in external walls can be filled with a patent insulating material at the time of construction.

Partition walls. The wall between the existing house and the new extension clearly needs a link — such as a door or opening of sorts. Since this wall probably bears a load, it must be tackled with caution. If you wish to remove all — or a large part — of it a rolled steel joist (RSJ) will have to be built in to support the load, and the foundations may well have to be underpinned.

An obvious place for a new door is where there is an existing window. The general rule here is that you can extend a window opening to almost any depth without extra strengthening, but extending the width means putting in a lintel to bear the weight of the wall above.

Arches are very decorative, but you must be certain that the wall either side is sufficiently strong to withstand the pressure from the wall above. As with all constructional matters, unless you have some technical knowledge of building it is advisable to consult the experts.

Air bricks are often set low in existing external walls. If the new extension is going to obstruct them, an alternative means of ventilating that part of the house wall must be incorporated in the new building.

Roofs are a specialist subject. But whatever type you have will need good insulation and proper guttering. Where a new roof surface abuts an old, the flashing (material that bridges the gap between two surfaces) must be sound and waterproof. Even a hairline crack is sufficient to let in damp — a building's biggest enemy.

Ceilings can be plaster board with a setting coat of plaster, which will require painting. Or just plaster board decorated with a single coat of one of the new patent finishes.

Timber cladding is an attractive if more expensive alternative, and can be put up by amateur decorators. Accoustic tiles are an excellent means of covering the ceiling and at the same time deadening the noise in, for example, a children's rumpus room.

'Wet' construction is a term used to describe building with materials made by mixing with water — such as plaster, cement and mortar. Hundreds of gallons of water can go into the construction of just a small area — and this water must be allowed to dry out before decorating with a hard paint such as gloss, or covering with· a plastic-coated paper. To cover wet walls with either of these two surfaces would cause the moisture to stay in the walls and do great damage at a later date. Emulsion paint, on the other hand, allows moisture to dry out through it. The drying out process can take as long as six months. In hot climates it may have to be 'inhibited'; otherwise the rapid drying of the exposed surface while the under-layer is still wet may lead to cracks.

The opposite to 'wet' construction is **'dry' construction** – using materials such as timber, plaster board (without a setting coat of plaster), dry stone or various patent materials. Actual construction is quicker with dry materials, and these can be decorated over at once.

Before building. If you have a mortgage, you must normally consult your mortgagees before undertaking any major alteration to the house, and obtain their permission. You must also check on your local building, fire and drainage regulations, which vary from area to area. Do not put up any structure without making certain that you have obtained the necessary permission to go ahead – or you may have to tear your handiwork down!

Dealing with builders. If you are employing builders direct, without the services of an architect or surveyor, shop around for estimates – which can vary enormously. Safeguard your money by getting a written estimate of the cost itemized down to the smallest detail; this is particularly useful in the event of any dispute once building is completed. And allow an emergency sum of at least an eighth over and above the estimated total for the building (up to a third to be really on the safe side), since it always seems to work out more expensively than planned.

It is a good idea to write a time clause into your contract with the builder, either awarding a bonus for completion of the work on time or imposing a penalty on the builder for each extra day the work takes.

Insurance. Check that the builders are fully insured against damage to the property during extending. And, when the work has been done, re-insure your house to its new value.

The best time to build is in the summer when weather conditions will allow the work to be completed quickly, to dry out quickly and to suffer the minimum of damage.

The site. Your choice of site may be somewhat limited by the area available for expansion, the shape of the existing house and the contours of the land around it. For example, if you live on a hill it is best to build along the contours of the land to avoid having steps inside the house and either extensive digging out of land or excessive building up of walls to match the various levels.

Try to choose a southern aspect for a living room extension; an eastern aspect for a bedroom (to catch the morning sun); and put nothing (except an artist's studio, which requires a constant light) facing north.

Types of extension. The cheapest is probably the *all-glass* variety, which anyone good with his hands could erect himself. The type of glass to use is glazing for factories: this is very light, and generally comes in standard sections, with t-shaped metal frames, though it could just as well be built with made-to-measure timber frames. Most manufacturers can supply the necessary weather proofing for the exterior. You will need a concrete sub-floor and foundations (not a suspended timber floor, since the framework of the extension is unlikely to be strong enough to support this).

For anyone who does not take to the idea of do-it-yourself, a local builder would probably tackle the job. But since this is not the kind of work he is accustomed to, you may do better to approach roofing contractors, who work with glass most of the time.

The advantages of glass are that it is quick and easy to erect, which makes it cheap. And it lets in and magnifies the sun. It is also very attractive (there is tinted glass on the market). However, it can get over-hot in summer and be cold in winter; and, unless the extension is well away from the road, there might be a noise problem. Double-glazing will help to lessen noise and to stop heat loss, too.

After glass, *timber* is probably the cheapest form of extending. This is a 'dry' construction – which means that you do not have to wait for the new building to dry out before decorating – and it is quick and clean to build. Most timber extensions are fairly light in weight and, since heat retention relies largely on density of wall, they need good insulation against the elements.

Timber usually requires a proper sub-floor of hardcore and concrete. And, when working out your

EXTENSIONS: A GLOSSARY

budget, take into account that wood used externally demands a certain amount of regular maintenance, such as stripping and painting or oiling approximately every three years.

Extensions made of *concrete or lightweight blocks* can prove inexpensive to assemble. The basic material is cheaper to buy than brick, and quicker to put up because of its larger unit size. These are 'wet' construction buildings, as the blocks are joined together with mortar. The surface outside needs rendering to give a reasonable appearance, while the interior surface needs plastering.

These blocks make sturdy buildings and, reinforced where necessary, can take any weight of roof or floor. Matching up rendering is not a difficult job, so this is a good way of extending a house which has been rendered.

Pre-fabricated kits. A number of manufacturers make extensions in kit form for amateurs to assemble themselves. These come complete with roofing, provision for electricity (although the circuit should be installed by a qualified engineer) and guttering and, in some cases, foundations and a suspended timber floor. (Where this last does not apply, you will have to lay a sub-floor of hardcore, damp-proofing and concrete. The kits have clear assembly instructions, and come in a wide variety of sizes and styles, with a choice of door and window fittings and finishes.

Generally speaking, a kit will work out cheaper than an extension involving architect's fees and builder's charges — even if you employ others to put it up for you instead of doing the assembling yourself.

Brick extensions are definitely a class above concrete, and proportionately more expensive. However, they do generally add more to the value of your house.

Like concrete, brick is a 'wet' construction and needs plastering on the inside. The process is lengthy but results in a very durable building, requires less maintenance and is less susceptible to damage than glass or timber. The framework will take any kind of roof or flooring, including a suspended timber floor on joists with air space beneath.

Matching the colour of old and new bricks can be quite difficult, but here your local builders' merchant should be able to help. He may have a library of samples, and can probably get a brick to match from the same manufacturers. This will be a darker shade initially to allow for weathering. To hide the join between a line of old bricks and a line of new, you can run a drainpipe down it. And if, in six months' time, the new bricks have not weathered in, there is always the admittedly rather drastic remedy of painting the whole of the exterior with one of the patent materials.

Stone or flint-faced cottages are possibly the most tricky types of dwelling to extend, since retaining the character of the building usually requires a perfect match of materials. Again, the local builders' merchant may be able to help, and a local craftsman who is versed in the eccentricities of the particular material will do the best construction job.